CHINA FOCUS

MODERN CHINA

Edited by Marta Segal Block

Heinemann Library
Chicago, Illinois

Customer Service   888–454–2279

Visit our website at www.heinemannlibrary.com

Designed by Richard Parker and Manhattan Design
Printed by China Translation Printing Services

12 11 20 09 08
10 9 8 7 6 5 4 3 2 1

Library of Congress Cataloging-in-Publication Data
Block, Marta Segal.
   Modern China / Marta Segal Block. -- 1st ed.
      p. cm. -- (China Focus)
   Includes bibliographical references and index.
   ISBN-13: 978-1-4329-1215-4 (hc)
   1. China--History--20th century--Juvenile literature. I. Title.
   DS774.B56 2008
   951.05--dc22
                              2007049474

Acknowledgments
The publishers would like to thank the following for permission to reproduce photographs:
©The Art Archive pp. **8** (Private Collection/Marc Charmet), **10** (British Museum); ©Art Directors & Trip (A. Tovy) p. **40**; ©Bridgeman Art Library pp. **9** (American Museum of Natural History, New York, USA, photo ©Boltin Picture Library), **16** (Archives Charmet/Private Collection), **17** (Private Collection); ©Chris Fairclough p. **38 (left)**; ©Corbis pp. **6** (Keren Su), **13** (Jose Fuste Raga), **20** (Bettmann), **22**, **23** (Hulton-Deutsch Collection), **27** (Bettmann), **24 (top)** (Dorothea Lange), **34** (Peter Turnley), **36** (Wally McNamee), **37** (epa/Pool/Alex Hofford), **38 (right)** (Howard Davies); ©Getty Images pp. **11** (Getty Images/IZA Stock), **19** (Hulton Archive), **24 (bottom)** (Hulton Archive), **26** (China Photos), **30** (Hulton Archive), **31** (Hulton Archive), **33** (Hulton Archive), **41** (AFP/Peter Parks); ©Mary Evans Picture Library p. **14**; ©PA Photos (AP) p. **35**; ©Pearson Education Ltd (Debbie Rowe) p. **12**; ©Peter Newark pp. **18**, **28**, **29**, **32**; ©Photolibrary pp. **5** (Daniel Cox), **7** (Panorama Media (Beijing) Ltd.

Cover photograph of Chinese soldiers parading in front of Mao Zedong's portrait (Peking, 1973) reproduced with permission of ©Getty Images (Roger Viollet/J. Culnieres).

The publisher would like to thank Tony Allan and David Downing for additional material.

Contents

Some words are printed in bold, **like this**. You can find out what they mean by looking in the glossary.

China Today

China is a huge country. Approximately 1.3 billion people live in a country that is more than 3 million square miles (9 million square kilometers). China shares a **border** with 14 different countries. One in every five people on Earth lives in China. More people live in China than in any other country. By 2020, China will probably have a population of 1.4 billion people.

The large space and number of people who live there make China very important to the world, **economically** and **politically**. China also is important to the world culturally. China has one of the oldest civilizations. Many items that we use every day, such as paper, were first invented in China.

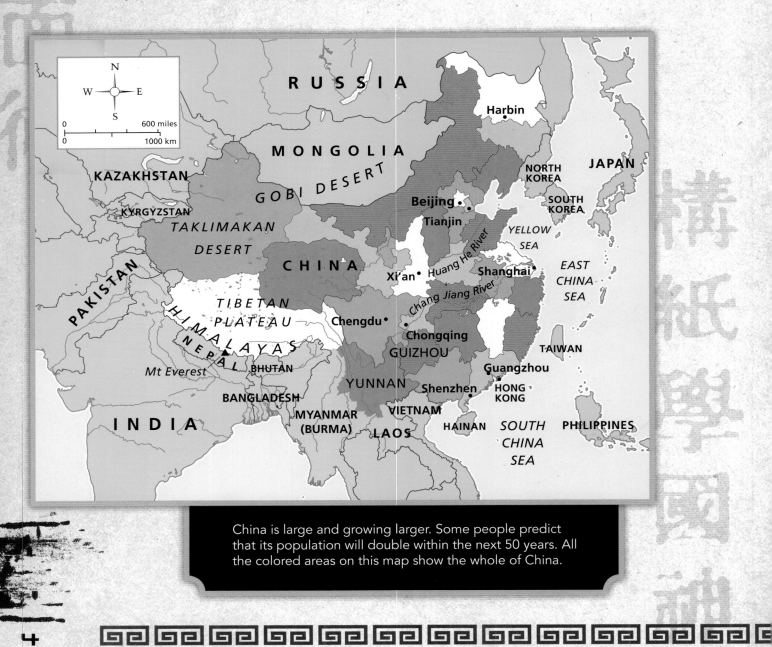

China is large and growing larger. Some people predict that its population will double within the next 50 years. All the colored areas on this map show the whole of China.

CHINESE ANIMALS

China does not just have a large population of people. Thirteen percent of the world's total population of birds and mammals are in China as well. Seventy-two kinds of mammals and 99 kinds of birds are found only in China. Several of China's animals are endangered, including the Giant Panda, the South China tiger, and the Chang River dolphin.

The Giant Panda is a symbol of China. Only 1,600 Giant Pandas are left in the wild. Several hundred more are in zoos and other protected areas.

Chinese language

In Chinese, words are written using symbols or characters, rather than letters. There are several different **dialects** of Chinese spoken throughout the country. There is a standard language known as *putonghua* (common language). English speakers often refer to this as Mandarin Chinese. Since Chinese is written differently from English, you often will see Chinese words spelled differently in different places. Sometimes, the words will look so different that they seem to not even be the same words. For example, the city of Beijing, China's capital, used to be spelled Peking in English. This book uses a system called Pinyin to write Chinese words. This is the Chinese government's preferred way of writing Chinese words in English letters.

The geography of China

Since China is so large, there is no one description of its landscape. China slopes down from the Himalayan Mountains to the Pacific Ocean. In the west, the mountains rise to high peaks. The middle of China is covered with grasslands and deserts, including the Gobi Desert. Most of China's people live in the east, where the green lowlands slope down to the sea.

China's rugged terrain means that the country's large population depends on food that is grown on just 10 percent of the land. Agriculture has always been an important part of the economy.

These giant snow sculptures were made in the northern city of Harbin, which has very cold winters.

For much of its history, China's geography, and the attitudes of its rulers, **isolated** it from much of the rest of the world. The famous Great Wall of China was first joined together in 221 BCE as a way of keeping outsiders out of China. China is no longer as isolated as it used to be. This is just one of the fascinating changes happening in this amazing country.

In China's north, the winters are extremely cold. But in the south, summer temperatures can get as high as 100°F (38°C).

The government of China

China's official name is The People's Republic of China. The country adopted this name in 1949, after the Chinese **Communist** Party took over the country. China is a **totalitarian** state. That means that the government has all the power and does not have to listen to what the people want. The country is divided into 33 areas. Each area has its own local government. Twenty-two of the areas are known as **provinces**.

The national currency, or money, of China is called Renminbi Yuan (people's money). As a Communist country, China's economy is controlled by the government. However, the economy is quickly moving to become more like the economies of the United States and the United Kingdom. The changes in the economy are helping to change China's government.

China Before 1900

China is one of the world's oldest countries. Its recorded history goes back thousands of years. For centuries, China was ruled by different families. These families were known as **dynasties**. China was largely unknown and untouched by countries outside Asia.

According to Chinese legends, the god Fuxi was the first king. Fuxi had the upper body of a man and the tail of a dragon. His wife, Nugua, made the first people out of clay. Fuxi taught the people how to hunt and fish, raise animals, and breed silkworms. Even today, silk is an important part of China's **culture** and economy.

According to legend, Fuxi invented writing, fishing, and hunting.

BEIJING MAN

In the 1920s, archeologists discovered human bones while digging in a Chinese cave. These bones are known as "Beijing Man" (formerly known as "Peking Man"). Beijing Man is believed to have lived as long as 500,000 years ago.

Beijing Man used crude stone tools, ate nuts and berries, and cooked his food over a fire.

The Xia Dynasty

By 2000 BCE, people living in northern China were living in walled settlements. They used tools, and had developed a writing system that became the basis for Chinese writing. According to Chinese stories, the Xia Dynasty ruled at this time. The first Xia **emperor** is known as Yu the Great Engineer. Historians still cannot prove whether the Xia Dynasty was real, because people who lived during this time did not leave written records.

The Shang Dynasty

The Shang Dynasty became powerful around 1600 BCE. The Shang Dynasty is the first empire that left written records.

The Zhou Dynasty

In about 1050 BCE, the Shang Dynasty was overthrown by the Zhou. At one point, the Zhou ruled from Mongolia in the north to the Chang River valley and beyond in the south. This was a time of both violence and new ideas. The **philosophies** of **Confucianism** and **Daoism** were first developed at this time. Today, these philosophies are practiced in China and around the world. Great discoveries were made in the fields of math, medicine, and astronomy.

This bronze pot is from the Shang Dynasty era. It was used to hold wine on special occasions.

The traditional Chinese calendar sometimes is called the Yin Calendar or the agricultural calendar.

ABOUT DATES

In Western culture, dates usually are given as either BCE (sometimes written as BC) or CE (sometimes written as AD). The term BCE stands for "before the common era." These dates often seem "backward." The year 5 BCE is a date five years before the start of the common era. The year 10 BCE happened before the year 5 BCE.

The Chinese have two different calendars. The traditional calendar may have been in use for more than 4,000 years. It is said to have started during the Xia Dynasty. This calendar is used to figure out the dates of holidays, such as the Chinese New Year and other important events. However, the Chinese also use the Gregorian Calendar (the calendar you use). The Gregorian Calendar is known as the official calendar.

Qin Shi Huangdi

Qin Shi Huangdi was leader after the Zhou Dynasty. Qin Shi Huangdi believed that people were bad and needed strict laws to keep them in order. He tried to outlaw ideas with which he disagreed. He ordered that all books of literature and philosophy be destroyed. Qin Shi Huangdi left behind two great works: The Great Wall of China and the famous Terracotta Warriors.

This tomb of more than 7,000 life-size statues of soldiers and horses was discovered in 1974.

CONFUCIUS

Confucius (551—479 BCE) was a government official who believed he had a mission to bring peace to war-torn China. Confucius's philosophy stated that people were basically good and needed rulers who set a good example. Confucius traveled from area to area talking about his ideas for creating a peaceful society. These ideas were known as the "Way of Heaven." Confucius's ideas were not widely followed during his lifetime, but later they became part of the official teachings of the Chinese government.

THE FEMALE EMPEROR

Wu Zeitan (625–705 CE) was China's only female emperor. She was a great supporter of Buddhism, and ruled well during a mainly peaceful period. Like many male emperors she is also remembered for being ruthless with her rivals and enemies.

The Golden Age

The Han Dynasty ruled from 206 BCE to 220 CE, more than 400 years. During this time, art, education, and science became very important. The Han grew China's **territory** and trade in all directions. One of the most famous trade routes created was known as the Silk Road. Traders traveled this route from as far away as Rome. Buddhists also traveled this route and brought **Buddhism** into China.

The Middle Ages

The Han were followed by the Sui, the Tang, and the Song Dynasties. In 1279, a leader from Mongolia, Kublai Khan, overthrew the last parts of the Song Dynasty. China was now under foreign rule.

The Silk Road was long and difficult, passing through mountains and over deserts.

The Ming Dynasty

Mongolian rule was followed by the Ming Dynasty. The Ming emperors attempted to restore the glory days of the Song and Tang Dynasties. The Ming Dynasty was one of the few Chinese dynasties to reach out to other countries. Most of China's dynasties had considered outsiders to be uncivilized and avoided contact. The Ming Dynasty was followed by the Manchurians.

MARCO POLO

Marco Polo (1254–1324), his father, and his uncle were traders from Venice, Italy. In 1271, they traveled east to visit China. In 1275 they reached the **court** of the Mongolian emperor, Kublai Kahn. Marco Polo eventually became an official in the **Mongol** empire and took on the customs and languages of his new home. In 1298, Polo wrote a book about his travels, and about China. For a long time, this book was the main source of information Europeans had about China.

Marco Polo's book about China was written in prison in Venice. It has never been clear how much of the book is fact and how much is fiction.

The Opium Wars

A drug called opium, made from the poppy flower, became popular in China during the 1600s. By the 1800s, the British controlled the Chinese opium trade. China tried to prevent this, but a war in the late 1830s gave the British even more power over China.

After China's defeat in the Opium Wars, other powerful countries such as France, the United States, Russia, and Germany all demanded special rights for their own traders. These countries were given special rights in the "unequal treaties," signed by the Chinese government.

In the 1890s, China found itself at war with its Asian neighbor, Japan, over Korea. Japan was much smaller than China in land and population, but it had a more modern economy and army. When its forces defeated the Chinese, China's failure was obvious for all to see. Once the center of the world, China was now no longer the chief power, even in its own region.

During the 1890s, China was at war with its smaller, more organized neighbour, Japan.

FAMINE

At the root of China's problems in the 19th century was a population explosion. From 1741—1840, China's population tripled, but the food supply failed to keep up. The famine of 1877—1878 killed millions of people.

China 1900–1949

China's emperors had referred to China as "The Middle Kingdom," meaning that China was the center of the world. But the 1900s were a time of disasters. For long periods in its past, China had led the world in **technology** and culture. By 1900, China was at a low point. In the West, the **Industrial Revolution** was changing the way countries worked and traveled. China, however, did not change.

The Boxer Rebellion

In 1900, after the nation's defeat by the Japanese, gangs of youths joined a secret movement known as the Fists of Righteous Harmony. The Boxers, as the rebels became known, practiced a secret form of **martial arts** that they claimed could magically protect them from bullets.

A painting by a Western artist shows an international force fighting the Boxers.

The Boxers took control of Beijing. The **imperial** government not only failed to stop the Boxers, but it secretly lent its support. Several nations, including Great Britain, the United States, Germany, France, Russia, and Japan, sent troops to defeat it. This was the only time the ruling countries of the day worked together in such a way. The crushing of the Boxers by foreign troops was a huge embarrassment for the Chinese government.

The end of an empire

By the time of the Boxer Rebellion, the emperor was no longer in charge. His mother, the ageing Empress Dowager, ruled the country. She stubbornly resisted any policy changes that would reduce her powers.

This photograph shows the Empress Dowager. It was taken around 1903, just five years before her death.

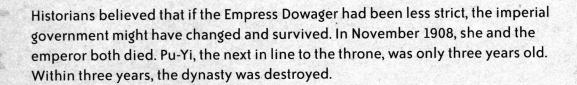

Historians believed that if the Empress Dowager had been less strict, the imperial government might have changed and survived. In November 1908, she and the emperor both died. Pu-Yi, the next in line to the throne, was only three years old. Within three years, the dynasty was destroyed.

Pu-Yi was the last emperor of China. He was forced to give up his right to the throne as a child. Later, the Japanese government set him up as a fake ruler in Manchuria.

The man who eventually destroyed the dynasty was from southern China. Sun Yatsen was born into a **peasant** family. He spent part of his childhood in Hawaii and then studied medicine in British-controlled Hong Kong. In Hong Kong, he became familiar with the way things were done in countries outside Asia. After trying and failing to get a job in the imperial administration, he became convinced that the only hope for China was to get rid of the emperors altogether and establish a **republic**.

The 10th uprising

Between 1895 and 1910, Sun's Republicans made nine attempts to start a revolution in China. All failed. But in 1911 they tried for a 10th time. This time, unhappy soldiers in the Chinese army joined them.

During the next two months, almost the entire country rose up to support the Republic. The advisers to Emperor Pu-Yi, who was still only five years old, realized Pu-Yi would have to **abdicate**. On January 1, 1912, the Republic of China was officially announced. Sun Yatsen was its first president. Thousands of years of imperial rule had come to an end.

Sun's presidency did not last long at all. After only 47 days, he was forced to hand over power to Yuan Shikai, a former war minister who was not very interested in **democracy**. Yuan died unexpectedly in 1916. The future of China was once again unclear.

Sun Yatsen spent several years in **exile**, living in the United States, Great Britain, and other places.

The fourth of May

While China was undergoing its own internal problems, much of the rest of the world was fighting World War I. The Treaty of Versailles, which ended the world war, gave Germany's **trading rights** in China to the Japanese. The Chinese were furious that the Western countries believed they had the right to do this. On May 4, 1919, Chinese students demonstrated in Beijing against the treaty. Most people in the West did not pay much attention to this demonstration, but it would prove to be important later on. As the 1920s went on, **poverty** and despair spread throughout China. The leaders of the May 4 demonstration became the leaders of the Chinese Communist Party.

Yuan Shikai tried to have himself declared emperor, but died before accomplishing this.

RISE, BROTHERS!

At the May 4, 1919 demonstration against the Japanese, student leaders offered a call to their country that ended this way:

"We earnestly hope that all agricultural, industrial, commercial, and other groups across the entire nation will call citizens' meetings to guard our **sovereignty** in foreign affairs and to get rid of the traitors at home. This is the last chance for China in her life and death struggle. Today we swear two solemn oaths with all our fellow-countrymen: (1) that China's territory may be conquered, but it cannot be given away; and (2) that the Chinese people may be massacred, but they will not surrender. Our country is about to be **annihilated**. Rise, brothers!"

A common cause

The Chinese Communist Party and the Nationalist Party (the party Sun Yatsen had created) were both interested in making China united. The two groups were happy to work together at first. Both bitterly opposed foreign interference in China, both sought an end to warlord power, and both wanted to reunite the nation. As long as Sun remained in charge of the Nationalists, the two parties also shared concerns about the poverty and bad living conditions in the country.

By 1926, however, the Nationalists had 200,000 members and the Communists only had 10,000. Many people in the Nationalist movement had become unhappy with the two groups being so close. Business people were unhappy about the **strikes** that were spreading through the cities. Landlords feared peasants would also cause problems. By 1927, the **alliance** came to a tragic, and bloody, end.

In the 1920s China suffered from poverty and famine. Clearly, people wanted a change.

Nationalist soldiers stop and search a suspected Communist during the Shanghai Purge.

The Shanghai Purge

In 1927, the Nationalist Army, under the leadership of Jiang Jieshi, defeated warlords who had been controlling parts of China. The Communists welcomed his success. However, Jiang saw the Communists as enemies. He unleashed his troops on them. Several thousand people suspected of being Communists were murdered in what was known as the Shanghai Purge.

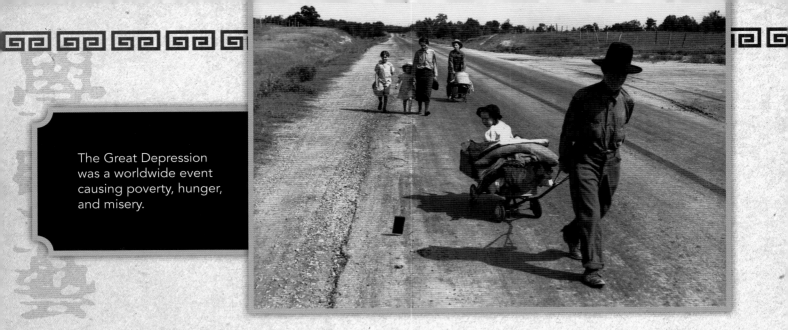

The Great Depression was a worldwide event causing poverty, hunger, and misery.

The 1930s

The **Great Depression** in the West also had a devastating effect on China. The depression, combined with a drought, a famine, and unhappy peasants, caused problems for Jiang Jieshi's government. Then in 1931, fresh trouble came from an unexpected place.

The Western powers (countries in Europe and North America) had been losing interest in China for some time. China's constant problems made the country difficult to do business with or to control. Japan, however, had maintained its interest in China, as it was eager to expand. By 1932, Japanese forces controlled the area of Manchuria, and set up the last emperor, Pu-Yi (now a grown man), as its head of state. Jiang did little to prevent this takeover, which angered the Chinese people and gave the Communists more popular support.

Jiang Jieshi (shown here in 1930) was the most powerful man in China from 1930–1949.

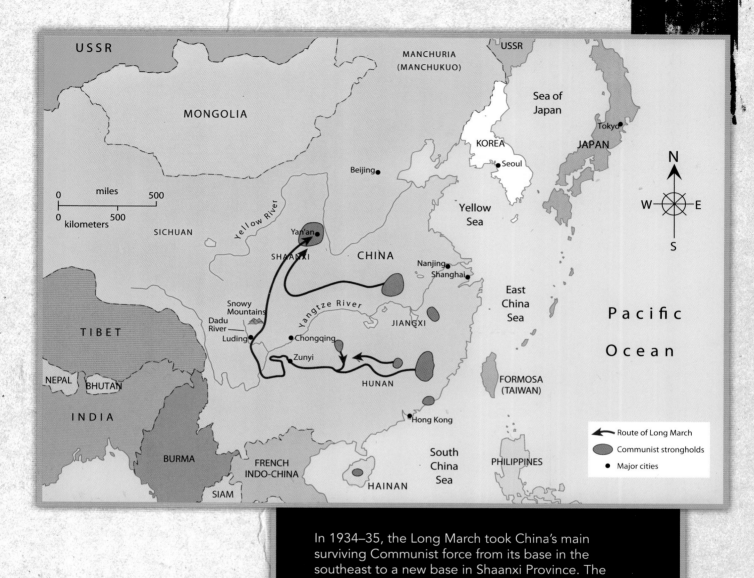

In 1934–35, the Long March took China's main surviving Communist force from its base in the southeast to a new base in Shaanxi Province. The march took a year.

The Long March

After the Shanghai Purge, the leaders of the Communist Party found themselves living as outlaws, often in hiding. By 1931, the largest group of Communists was located in the Jiangxi Province, led by a 36-year-old named Mao Zedong. The Chinese Communist Party was influenced heavily by the Communist government in the **Soviet Union**.

The Soviet Union later tried to take over the Chinese Communist Party. However, Mao's position of leadership was made strong by the Long March, a 6,213 mile (10,000 kilometer) march he took with Communist forces. He made this march to stop the Nationalist party from destroying his army.

China 1949–1988

In 1939, World War II broke out in Europe. At this point, China was divided essentially into three unequal sections. In the northwest, Mao was gaining ground. Japan (fighting on the side of the Germans) was famous for its horrible treatment of the Chinese. The Communists led successful small attacks against the Japanese, gaining support for themselves.

On October 1, 1949, Mao pronounced the foundation of the People's Republic of China. Mao continued the traditions of imperial times, by declaring the republic from the Gate of Heavenly Peace.

The Gate of Heavenly Peace, located in the Forbidden City, has been an important site in China for centuries.

Chairman Mao

Mao Zedong (1893–1976) was born into a wealthy farming family in Hunan Province in southeast China. At 16, he left home for school. His heroes were the warrior emperors of Chinese history, such as Qin Shi Huangdi. Mao was introduced to Communist ideas while working at Beijing University.

Early years

When Mao took over, the Nationalists fled to the island of Taiwan. This left mainland China united for the first time in more than 100 years. Most Chinese welcomed the end of fighting. Land **reform** meant that land was taken away from landowners, many of whom did not live there, and given to poor peasants.

In the cities, the new rulers took over newspapers, banks, transportation systems, gas, and electricity services. Government cheating was wiped out, as were many crimes. In both the city and the countryside, more than 1 million people were killed as a result of the reforms.

The Communist Party was the only political party allowed. Churches were closed and foreign **missionaries** forced out. Everyone was expected to follow the beliefs of the Communist Party.

No figure is more important in the history of modern China than Mao Zedong.

TIBET

In 1950, the Communists invaded Tibet, which had been independent from 1911 to 1950. The Buddhist people of Tibet bitterly resented the invasion. Today, Tibet is technically an independent region of China, but the people there still struggle for their independence.

The 1950s

During the Korean War (1950–1953), China had sided with the Soviet Union and the Communists in Korea. Although many Chinese soldiers died in the war, the war helped the Chinese gain international standing and respect. The years from 1953 to 1957 were very good for China economically.

In 1957, in response to events in the Soviet Union, and to China's success, Mao began to relax the rules against political disagreement in China. However, this period of increased debate soon ended.

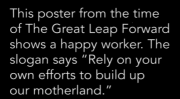

This poster from the time of The Great Leap Forward shows a happy worker. The slogan says "Rely on your own efforts to build up our motherland."

The Great Leap Forward

In 1958, Mao began a three-year plan known as The Great Leap Forward. The goal was to change life dramatically in China. Unfortunately, poor planning and bad weather brought drought and famine. Since people were afraid to tell Mao the truth about what was happening, bad decisions continued to be made. Millions of people starved. By late 1960, it was clear that Mao's plan had been a disaster. Because of this, Mao was forced to give more political power to two men, Liu Shaoqi and Deng Xiaoping. Both men were less strict than Mao.

This planned photo shows happy peasants celebrating a good harvest.

Cultural Revolution

Mao became convinced that the problems of the country were a result of people believing in traditional Chinese values and attitudes. In 1966, he set up a Cultural Revolution group to fight against traditional habits. He placed his wife, Jiang Qing, in charge of the group. College students who agreed with Mao began to call themselves the "Red Guard" and began destroying anything representative of the "Four Olds." The Four Olds were old culture, old ideas, old **customs**, and old habits.

Chaos continues

By 1967, the violence was getting out of hand. Foreigners were attacked and things were beginning to seem like the Boxer Rebellion. Mao ordered the Red Guard to stop their activities but it was two more years before the situation was brought under control. Thousands had died as a result. The Cultural Revolution officially came to an end in 1976.

China's Defense Minister, Lin Bao, came out of the situation with a lot of power. However, he died two years later in a plane crash. His death led to the rising of Zhou Enlai, and the return of Deng Xiaoping. Mao's wife, Jiang Qing, also remained politically powerful. She formed a group known by others as the Gang of Four, to keep the Cultural Revolution alive.

Schoolgirls read from *The Little Red Book* of Mao's thoughts.

China, the Soviet Union, and the United States

In the 1960s, China and its former friend, the Soviet Union, began to disagree and fight. The United States, seeing the Soviet Union as its main enemy, sided with China. In 1971, U.S. President Richard Nixon allowed China to join the **United Nations**. Before 1971, the Nationalist government, located in Taiwan, had been recognized by the United States and the United Nations as the official Chinese government. In 1972, Nixon made a visit to the Chinese mainland, recognizing Mao's government for the first time.

President Nixon visited the Great Wall of China during his 1972 visit. Nixon's trip signaled a change in relations between China and the United States.

WHAT IS COMMUNISM?

The word Communism comes from a French phrase meaning "belonging to all." The idea has a long history. Long before there were Communist parties or countries, there were people who believed in the simple idea of sharing ownership of society's resources. This would, in theory, lead to a kinder society where people would cooperate.

This is not the way Communism tends to be practiced today. In the modern world, Communist governments tend to have certain things in common. There usually is only one political party, and disagreement generally is not allowed. The economy is owned almost completely by the government. Other aspects of social life, such as education and entertainment, also are controlled by the government.

Advances in communications and travel mean that countries today interact with each other more than ever before. This means that in order to be successful, even Communist countries such as China and Cuba have had to adopt some principles of **capitalism**.

A careful balance

In 1976, both Zhou Enlai and Mao died. Within three years, Deng Xiaoping, now 74 years old, was given the title "Paramount Leader." The country was tired of the conflict and fighting. Deng was welcomed. In contrast to the Red Guard's "The Four Olds," Zeng began a program known as "The Four Modernizations," stressing the need to update industry, defense, technology, and agriculture. At the same time, Deng promoted "The Four Cardinal Principles," which all involved staying true to **Socialist** thought.

Following Mao's death, 1 million people attended his memorial gathering in Tiananmen Square. Thirteen years later, the Square would become known around the world for another reason.

Deng cared more about results than strict following of Communism. He once said "It doesn't matter if a cat is black or white, so long as it catches mice." He meant that having things work the way they are supposed to is more important than political views. Deng allowed people to go to other countries to study, and welcomed foreign businesses and advice into China.

Deng's balance between modern economy and traditional political views was not easy to maintain. In 1987, a wave of student protests erupted in China. In response, the Communist Party Secretary Hu Yaobang, who was known to be sympathetic to the protesters, was fired. What happened next would shock the world.

Under Deng's policies, workers who produced more could earn more. This policy was not in strict keeping with the ideas of Communism.

THE ONE CHILD POLICY

China's growing population reached 1 billion shortly after Deng took control. Deng decided to take action to reduce the growth rate. In 1979, he started a campaign to restrict families to just one child. Those who had more than one child were punished by fines and they lost some health and education benefits. The policy succeeded in cutting the **birth rate** by almost half. The policy is still in effect today, but is carried out differently in different areas of the country.

China 1989–2007

In 1989, Hu Yaobang, the fired Communist party official, died. As had happened following Zhou Enlai's death in 1976, demonstrators came to Tiananmen Square on the day of Hu's funeral to show their grief.

The government took no action at first, even though such demonstrations had been declared illegal. Then students set up tents in the square and announced that they were going on a hunger strike to demand change.

Student protesters crowded into Tiananmen Square in 1989.

For over a month, the protesters kept control of Tiananmen Square. Some people, led by Deng, wanted to send in the army. Other people were desperate to find a peaceful solution. Eventually the army was sent in, but even then the soldiers did not want to act against their fellow people. Thousands of Beijing citizens blocked their path, and the troops did not have orders to shoot their way through.

Meanwhile, the students in the square were becoming more outspoken. They built a copy of the Statue of Liberty. This was a symbol of their desire for democracy. Finally, troops moved in on the square. This time the soldiers had orders to shoot at the crowd. By dawn the following morning, the students had been moved out. It is thought that hundreds of students were killed or injured.

Eventually the army was ordered to deal violently with the protestors.

Sad victory

The fighting spread to other cities in China. Several hundred people were killed, many of them students. Thirteen years after Deng had encouraged protests, he was now the one facing demonstrations. He won the battle, but lost many of the brightest young people in China. These were the very people who could have helped in his modernization plans. Around the world, other countries blamed China for killing its own people.

More of the same

The Tiananmen Square disaster did not change the direction of government policy. Deng explained what had happened to the Chinese people as the work of a few bad people trying to destroy the nation's stability. Deng continued to follow a policy of political **repression**.

Economic reforms

While Deng did not want outside influence in politics, he did want it in economics. He continued to welcome expert help from other countries. This effort was helped by U.S. policy. The United States believed that the best way to encourage China to be more democratic was to encourage it to have contact with the outside world. The modernization program helped change life for many Chinese people. Between 1981 and 1991, China had increased trade and production.

U.S. president Bill Clinton accompanies Deng's successor, Jiang Zemin, as he reviews the troops. Throughout the 1990s, China pursued a policy of trading with the West.

Hong Kong was given back to China in 1997.

Deng's death

In 1997, Deng died at the age of 92. His chosen successor was the former mayor of Shanghai, Jiang Zemin. Jiang continued to follow Deng's economic and political policies, although he traveled abroad more than earlier leaders. He kept tight political control at home. Hu Jintao, the current leader of China, took over from Jiang Zemin in 2003. He has generally been keen to develop an untroubled relationship with the rest of the world.

The return of Hong Kong

Four and a half months after Deng's death, Hong Kong was returned to Chinese rule. Hong Kong had originally been taken by the British after the first Opium War in 1842, and the British rule there was a reminder of China's 19th-century weakness.

In 1898, Britain was given a 99-year lease on the land around Hong Kong. In 1984, Deng and British Prime Minister Margaret Thatcher signed an agreement for the return of the entire colony in 1997. In return, China promised to keep Hong Kong's existing economic and social system for at least 50 years. The colony was handed back on schedule.

China in the 21st century

Today, some areas of China are doing well economically while others continue to struggle. The nation also is being pulled in two directions politically. China is still trying to keep a balance of being open to the West economically, while maintaining tight political control.

China is a country of contrasts. The economy of cities is booming, while rural life remains difficult.

The new China

China is changing in many ways that in time may lead to demands for a more open and democratic society. More and more of the population lives in the cities, and people are better-educated and fed.

Population

Not all the developments in China are positive. Although the One Child Policy proved effective in slowing population growth, it still left the nation as the world's most populous, with 1.3 billion people. Of that total, more than a billion live on only one-sixth of the nation's land area, in the east and along the fertile river valleys, creating problems of overcrowding and pollution.

Olympics and scandals

In 2008, China will host the summer Olympic Games. This is just one symbol of China's growing importance in the world. However, another side of its growing importance can be seen in a series of recent scandals.

In 2002, **SARS**, a serious illness, broke out in the Guangdong Province and Hong Kong. The Chinese government's tradition of not letting its people, or foreigners, know about certain things made the situation worse. While the government claimed the illness was under control, the **World Health Organization** issued warnings about traveling to China.

In 2007, pet food that was made in China and sent to other countries was found to contain a poison. Many pets in the United States died because of the poison, and the food was taken off store shelves. In the same year, many toys made in China and sold abroad were found to contain the poison lead. These toys also had to be taken off store shelves.

In still another scandal, the U.S. Department of Defense accused the Chinese military of breaking in to the computers at the Pentagon, the department's headquarters. These scandals show that some of the problems in China remain. The Chinese government's interest in keeping secrets makes it hard for China to communicate with other countries. China wants to be part of the world economically, but not politically.

The Future of China

Changes in technology and communication have made the world a smaller place. China is no longer a mysterious country far off in the east. Modern, everyday life in China is much like it is anywhere else. People go to movies, talk on their cell phones, and eat at American restaurants.

Today, China is the world's largest producer of coal, steel, and cement. It is the second-largest user of energy. It is the third-largest importer of oil. During the past 15 years, China's **exports** have grown by huge amounts.

Just like the early Communists and Nationalists, China's government today is struggling to find ways to blend modern life with traditional values and culture. Whatever the future holds for China, it is unlikely that it will ever return to the isolated days of its past.

China is a country that is moving forward while taking pride in its past.

Chinese food is available throughout the rest of the world, and now food from other countries is available in China.

COFFEE, HAMBURGERS, AND TRADITION

The conflict China feels between growing Western influence and its own traditions can be seen in a recent conflict over Starbucks, the U.S. coffee store chain. Starbucks opened a store in the Forbidden City, the former home of the emperors. Although the Chinese government officially condemns its imperial past, many Chinese consider the Forbidden City to be the cultural heart of China. The public outcry at having the U.S. chain store in such an important place caused the store to close. Despite the closing of this store, however, sales continue to be good at other Starbucks stores in China. Similar controversies have been brought up over McDonald's and Kentucky Fried Chicken.

Timeline

1900	The Boxer Rebellion takes place.
1911	Revolution ends China's last imperial dynasty.
1912	The Republic of China is announced with Sun Yatsen as its president, soon replaced by Yuan Shikai. The Nationalist Party is set up.
1919	May 4 movement of student demonstrations takes place.
1921	First Congress of Chinese Communist Party meets.
1927	The Shanghai Purge takes place.
1930	Famine, following three years of drought, kills millions of Chinese.
1932	The Japanese announce the kingdom of Manchukuo in the occupied areas, with the last Qing emperor, Pu-Yi, as its ruler.
1934	Communists begin the Long March.
1945	World War II ends.
1946	Civil war breaks out between Nationalists and Communists.
1949	Communist troops capture Beijing and Nanjing. The People's Republic of China is established, with Mao Zedong as its leader.
1950	The Red Army invades Tibet. China and the Soviet Union sign a friendship treaty. China enters the Korean War.
1952	China launches the Five Year Plan.
1958	The Great Leap Forward begins.
1960	Widespread famine starts the end of the Great Leap Forward. The Soviet Union withdraws all advisers from China.
1966	Liu and Deng are criticized. The Cultural Revolution breaks out.
1969	Fighting breaks out on the Chinese-Soviet border.
1972	U.S. President Nixon visits China.

1976 The death of Zhou Enlai starts the Tiananmen Square demonstrations. Mao Zedong dies. The Gang of Four are arrested.

1978 Deng Xiaoping emerges as leader.

1984 China and Britain issue a joint declaration on the future of Hong Kong.

1986 The government shows a tough response to protests in Chinese universities.

1989 Pro-democracy demonstrations end badly in Tiananmen Square.

1997 Deng Xiaoping dies. Hong Kong is returned to Chinese control by Britain.

2003 SARS breaks out in China.

2007 There are several scandals involving contamination of pet food and toys.

2008 China hosts the 2008 Summer Olympics.

Glossary

abdicate voluntarily give up power

alliance group of people or countries working together

annihilate wipe out

birth rate the number of births within a population

border division between two countries

Buddhism religion based on the teachings of the Buddha

Capitalist economy based on the idea that the market will decide what is and is not valuable; person who believes this is the best government

Communist government based on the teachings of Karl Marx; person who believes in the teachings of Marx

Confucianism belief system started by Confucius

court where the emperor lives

culture actions and beliefs of a society

custom usual way of behaving in a certain situation

Daoism religion based on the ideas of Laozi

democracy government where people elect their rulers

dialect variety of a language that is spoken in a particular region

dynasty families who rule an area for more than one generation

economy system under which a country creates, sells, and buys products

emperor ruler who has total power, like a king

exile forced to live outside one's own country

export goods sold to another country; to sell to another country

Great Depression worldwide event in the 1930s that destroyed the economies of many countries, causing poverty and hardship

imperial to do with the emperor

Industrial Revolution movement that started in Great Britain in the 18th century that changed the economy of many countries

isolated separated from others

martial arts traditional training of body and mind to keep self-control

missionary person sent overseas to spread their religion

Mongol person from Mongolia, a country next to China

peasant worker who works on land raising food, but does not own the land

philosophy way of thinking about the world

political related to the way a country is run or its government

poverty lacking in basic needs such as food, clothing, and shelter

province area of a country, similar to a state

reform change

repress hold back

republic country where people have the right to choose their leaders

SARS virus that affects the lungs and can be deadly

Socialist person who believes in Socialism. Socialism is an ideology that promotes ownership of the means of production by the state.

sovereignty power of a state

Soviet Union group of communist countries, led by Russia, which existed from 1922 to 1991; also known as the USSR

strike to stop working, eating, or another important function in order to bring about change

technology scientific knowledge used in practical ways

territory land under control of a ruler

totalitarian form of government that demands agreement with a set of ideals

trading rights country's right to do business in a foreign country

United Nations organization of the world's countries to keep peace and order internationally

World Health Organization (WTO) international organization designed to administer trade between countries

Further Information

Books

Field, Catherine. *Nations of the World: China*. Chicago: Raintree, 2003.

Guile, Melanie. *Culture in China*. Chicago: Heinemann, 2003.

March, Michael. *Country File: China*. North Mankato, MN: Smart Apple Media, 2004.

Olson, Nathan. *China*. Mankato, MN: Capstone, 2005.

Places to visit

Many museums have good Chinese collections. Here are some of the more famous ones:

The Metropolitan Museum of Art
1000 5th Ave at 82nd Street
New York, NY 10028-0198
(212) 535-7710   www.metmuseum.org

The Art Institute of Chicago
111 South Michigan Ave
Chicago, IL 60603
(312) 443-3600   www.artic.edu

Asian Art Museum of San Francisco
200 Larkin Street
San Francisco, CA 94102
(415) 581-3500   www.asianart.org

Websites

Ask Asia

www.askasia.org/kids

The Asia Society's site provides information for students and teachers on Asian countries.

Official Chinese Government Website

www.china.org.cn

This official website is for English speakers. This website presents images and information about China that the Chinese government wants the rest of the world to see.

The CIA Factbook

www.cia.gov/library/publications/the-world-factbook/index.html

The CIA factbook has information on every country in the world. This website is run by the U.S. government.

Index